Winds Of A Silent Song

A collection of poetry

Abhishek Walwaikar

BookLeaf Publishing

India | USA | UK

Made with ❤ on the BookLeaf Publishing Platform
www.bookleafpub.in
www.bookleafpub.com

Dedication

To Araina, my brightest inspiration,
To Amruta, my steady anchor,
To Aai, my foundation.
And the Almighty, my pole star.

Preface

In the clamour and rush everyday life, we often overlook the subtle emotions and thoughts that shape our life experiences. Winds of a Silent Song, my debut collection of poems is born from the desire to capture these hidden moments, those silent whispers of the heart that often go unheard. Through these poems I ask you to pause, to reflect upon and reconnect with these melodies of our inner world. Through exploration of love, beauty, longing and introspection of everyday moments, I hope to evoke a sense of shared emotions. My intention is to offer a quite reminder that within the chaos, there exist a hidden reservoir of emotions, waiting to be acknowledged .

These poems are a reflection of the silent murmurs of my heart. As you journey through them, I invite you to listen closely - to the winds of a silent song that carries the unheard echoes of our hearts. May you find peace, inspiration and perhaps a bit of yourself within these verses.

Thank you for allowing me to share this book and journey with you.
— Abhishek Walwaikar

Acknowledgements

First Crush,
First Love,
First Heartbreak,
A Friend, who save my life,
My loving wife,
One Mentioned and not.
Ones I never forgot.

This book is a culmination of many people and moments that have shaped my journey . I am deeply grateful to all those who have been a quiet inspiration along the way. Whose influence is ever-present, your inspiration is real hand writing these words. Everyone who has stood my me in big or small way, thank you for being part of this journey.

With heartfelt gratitude,

—Abhishek Walwaikar

1. First Love

A flutterling heart and blushing cheek,
A feeling so new, makes me weak,
My mind consumed by just one face,
A charmer's face, a sweet embrace.

Upon my lips a name now dwells,
In secret scripts, my notebook tells,
I steal a glance, a stolen gaze,
Entranced by you, lost in your maze.

2. Firefly

Her laughter, a melody in quiet's embrace,
A warmth that lingers, a tranquil space.
Her eyes aglow,with dreams yet untold,
In her radiance, my love unfolds.

In twilight's haze, she dances with grace,
A firefly in motion, a celestial trace.
Amidst whispers of stars, her spirit takes flight,
In her presence, darkness surrenders to light.

3. Hope

Amidst the ashes and smoke,
A beautiful flower, I saw grow.
A Daisy, its petals white as snow,
A symbol of hope in a place of woe.

A beauty, in the garden of death,
The flower brought a fresh breath.
A life in bloom, a symbol so true,
Even in death, life can renew.

4. Shall we fight, my love ?

Shall we fight , my love tonight ?
In this silly, playful light.
Not with swords or angry glares,
But words, pranks and dares.

Lets duel with words that softly sting,
Teasing smiles, they will surely bring.
Your weapon's wit, mine is gentle charm,
No one's here to do real harm.

In the end, its all a game,
This sparring dance without a name.
But when the quarrel's lost its spark,
Lets laught and kiss beneath the dark.

5. Mrignayani

Her gaze, a whisper in the enchanted night,
In her eyes, the stars take flight.
In those depths, secrets of forests unfold,
A tale of beauty, in every glance told.

7. Shadows of Solitude

A crowd moves on life's path, I see,
Yet loneliness engulfs silently.
Fragile tiles, like toys of clay,
In an instant, they may break away.

This world appears a vibrant fete,
But sorrow lurks, hearts wounded great.
Once smiles adnorned each visage bright,
Dreams embraced, find solace in night.

Now shattered dreams, their sleeps demise,
Alone they stand with tearful eyes.
In the paths of life, the crowd will sway,
Yet loneliness prevades, night and day.

Note: This poem is written as a tribute to the beautiful
song 'Dekhiye Toh Lagta Hai,'
penned by Javed Akhtar for the Indian television show
Tanha (1997).

6. Twilights Date

In whispers soft, I share my plea,
To stroll with you, sit beneath the tree.
With twilight near, the world grows still,
As moonlight dances over the hill.

In tender light, your smile so bright,
Turns dusk to dawn, pure delight.
Hand in hand, time drifts from sight,
This evening feels like purest light.

8. Your Absence

Even in our sepration,
there is your presence.
Even in your absence,
there is our love.

9. Heart's Silence

In quiet moments, our hearts connect,
No need for words, our feelings reflect.
Eyes meet, singing love's silent song,
Hushed lips, feelings so strong.

Unspoken stories in each gaze we find,
Wordless conversations of heart and mind.
This precious bond, where silence holds sway,
Into our worlds, love found its way.

10. Beloved's Pain

In shadows of my heart, a pain does hide,
Watching her, I am teary-eyed.
Beneath the moon's soft silver glow,
My heart aches as sorrow ebbs and flow.

My beloved, lost in life's despair,
Her eyes dimmed, burdened beyond repair.
A face so sad, detached from light,
Within my soul, storms take flight.

To find her alone, weary and worn,
Gazing into the abyss, my heart is torn.
Her solitude, a broken heart in chain,
A void that echoes with unspoken pain.

11. Love Story

They meet,
They laugh,
They love,
They cry,
They fight,
They fall,
They heal,
They stand,
They grow,
Thcy age,
They endure.

12. Whispers of the Wind

Why the stars shimmer, far up high ?
Why does the river softly sigh ?
Why does the wind in trees reply.
With secrets old, yet never told?

Why does the monsoon kiss the clay,
That holds the scent of yesterday?
In mango groves, where echoes lie,
Of tales that time lets slip—goodbye.

13. Twilight's Love

In silvered strands and wrinkles deep,
Time's journey traces, memories to keep.
Old age unfolds its tender grace,
A tale of wisdom, etched on their face.

Through faded hues of yesteryears,
Love emerges, conquering tears.
In twlight's glow two hearts entwine,
Find solace in love divine.

14. Betrayal

I loved you more than my faith,
I adored you more than God,
I respected you more than the holy words,
I sought you beyond immortality,
I believed in you more than myself,
Alas ! the broken I, now repents.

15. A Broken Flower

A broken flower on the ground,
Its petals scattered all around.
Once a thing of beauty grand,
Now a sight, hard to withstand.

Though the broken flower may seem,
A distant memory, shattered dreams.
Its beauty still lingers in the air,
A sweet fragrance, reminds us to dare.

To dare to live, to love, to be,
To embrace life, full and free.
Like broken flower, we too,
Can find strength, anew.

16. Forbidden Love

My heart it beats for a secret love,
For she, the one I can't possess.
Her beauty, pure as an innocent dove,
Her wits, a blade that does impress.

Norms dicate whats deemed right,
And love like ours, it can't be so.
I fight these feelings tight,
And keep my love for her below.

Oh! she haunts my every though,
Like cool shade on a summer's day,
And in my heart, a longing wrought,
To tell her all, I wish to say.

17. Lost at Sea

At the edge of the world, I stand,
Gazing into the endless blue.
Where the sky and sea whispers secrets,
In a language only the heart understands.

Time dissolves in the rhytms of waves,
Each crest a breath, each trough a sigh.
Solitude wraps its gentle arms around me,
Not in loneliness, but in quiet reflection.

The vast ocean, a mirror to my soul,
Reflects the boundless thoughts within.
And in the sea's gentle embrace,
I am both, lost and found.

18. Whispering Dreams

In hope's embrace, desires unfold,
Unfulfilled yet, they turn to gold.
Like whispered secrets in twilight's gleam,
Dreams untouched—an eternal theme.

The moon, a distant, radiant sphere;
If in our hands, would it still appear?
Its mystic charm—where would it reside,
Held too close, does its beauty hide?

Longings unquenched, they light our way,
A flame within, by night and day.
In pursuit of all not attained,
We find life's essence, unrestrained.

19. Life's Garden

In a lush garden, on a summer's day,
Happiness, Love, Sadness came to play,
Jealousy and Anxiety, hastily gathered around,
With Kindness and Greed waiting, they found.

Happiness danced with joy and glee,
Skipping and laughing carefree,
Love sang songs of passion and desire,
Twinkling eyes , putting heart on fire.

Sadness sat in a corner alone,
Brooding and crying in a mournful tone,
Jealousy eyed Love with a green-eyed glare,
Greed scheming and plotting, envious air.

Anxiety paced with worries and fears,
Fidgeting and stressing, shedding tears,
Kindness smiled and spread God's will,
Lifting spirits, gentle and still.

Sadness found solace in Kindness's embrace,
Finding comfort in a warm, caring place.
Jealousy's plot failed one by one,
As Love and Happiness won everyone.

Anxiety found peace with Happiness in the air,
Learning to forsake worries and care.
Greed's hoard eroded, its joy fleeting,
Nothing was gained in competing.

In the end Kindness never failed,
With love and Happiness, it prevailed.
Now no gloomy shadows or strife,
The garden bloomed, with life.

20. Desert Rose

Through shifting sands, her roots entwine the earth,
In solitude, she finds her boundless worth.
Her fierce beauty, soft yet rare,
A desert rose, beyond compare.

21. Beloved's Embrace

Walking in the mist of clouds,
In the oceans of flowers, I lay,
Where sweet scent of honey abounds,
Where the bees jump and play.

I long to rest in your arms,
Beneath the mango tree,'
Away from life and far from death,
Till my bones and flesh are no more.

Walking in the mist of clouds,
In the oceans flowers, I lay.